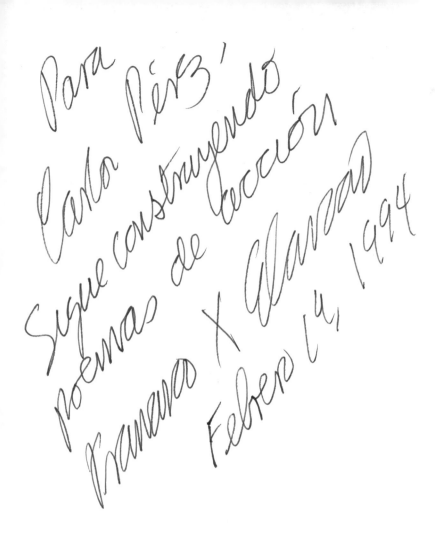

Para
Carlo Pérz,
Sigue construyendo
poemas de occión

Mariano X Alarcón
Febrero 14, 1994

No Golden Gate for Us

Francisco X. Alarcón

Pennywhistle Press
Santa Fe
1993

Poems from this collection have previously appeared in the following publications: *Centroamérica en el alma*: "Continental"; *City on a Hill*: "Chant," "L.A. Prayer"; *El Tecolote Literario*: "'Mexican' Is Not a Noun"; *Guadalupe Review*: "Silence"; *New Chicana/Chicano Writing*: "Extranjero/ Foreigner," "Isla Mujeres," "We Are Trees"; *Poetry USA*: "Grandson's Rage"; *Puerto del Sol*: "Casa Materna," "Callejeros"; *Quarry West*: "No Golden Gate For Us"; *Revista Mujeres*: "The X in My Name"; *Tattoos*: "Banderas/Flags," "Eros," "Raíces/Roots."

Printed in the United States of America
by Publishers Press, Salt Lake City

ISBN: 0-938631-16-0

For additional copies, address orders to: Pennywhistle Press
P. O. Box 734
Tesuque, NM 87574

Note: Poems with the following mark: ∿
at the bottom of the page are continued on the next page.

Contents

a la memoria
de mis abuelos

Introduction

This is the black and white hieroglyph of (Re)-possession—words that re-call, re-decipher and re-integrate in a new fashion that which has been sabotaged, disassembled and stripped: America and its guardians. It is a matter of spirit more than structure; history with sparkles, more than with chronology—words with the power of windstorm and being. I will call this collection a speakerly-codex and the poems, sign-speakers.

The sign-speakers appear in various shades and intonations of light and voice traversing through time, body and mineral. At times, in a singular aspect, we sense solitudes, darknesses —going through the void in order to recollect and conjure. For this there are various requirements; the sign-speakers tell us: silence, or better yet, a quiescent death of the things we all are accustomed to in our lives. Then we go inside, it seems, into these stilled orbs to find the heart willing to explode; a heart must be ready to burst, then wonder, this is another intrinsic law; this is how to gather the new land and its peoples. This is how we must chart the new coordinates of living; our task is to trek continuously; the sign speakers point in this direction: the open syntax, the accelerated stanzaic motion and the loosened caesura (if we can still use these terms at all) and the verticality of the sign-speakers as *stelae* perhaps, all serve to guide us quickly, to gain internal knowledge and external velocities of new being. And as we go and if we gain entry through this new motion, we will also discard the oppressive forms of "reading" the world in order to take on a new grammar of liberation.

As a whole, the sign-speakers act as a shamanic set of gestures, a smoothing of the ground, an inhalation of the solar winds and exhalation of the debris of the land's flesh. The eyes are fixed on the navel; everything must come back to its center (Re)-possessed and then carried back with new properties; the sign-speakers and their breath whorls call upon trees, dogs, skin, roots, bedrooms and the marching multitudes. They shout out: it is time to awaken the dead. These "poems" are the vertical incense, the tall fire that threads us to the Milky Way—since it is all at our reach. Our voices will come back to us in rock-forms and "stranger"-forms. This is how we shall heal. This is how our body shall gain its erotic sheaths again—the nipples, the viscera of the heart, the seeking skin and the shimmering voice.

Everything is delicate, so we must hold each other, embrace, or we may fall back in an instant, to the numbed-world, the stolen land, raped. Yet, we must remember that for the shaman, delicate gestures are loud acts that (Re)-possess, such as birthing screams or animal phonemes. I suggest that you come to Francisco X. Alarcon's speakerly-codex in a new way as you might want to come to a new California and a new America—knock on the door, even if it looks like your house, stand in readiness for an old woman to answer, dressed in black, shadowy, gripping a broom; stand ready to reach inside yourself, become speechless, lose everything at the door, then enter. This is where you were born, remember?

Juan Felipe Herrera
Southern Illinois University
November 1992

FIRST POSSESSION OF CALIFORNIA

"I bring with me many acts of taking possession of all that Coast. And by the situation of the River (the Colorado River), and the height which I took, I find that that which the Masters and Pilots of the Marquesse (Hernán Cortés) took is false, and that they were deceived by 2 degrees, and I have sailed beyond them above 4 degrees. I sailed up the River 85 leagues, where I saw and learned all the particulars before mentioned, and many other things; whereof when it shall please God to give me leave to kiss your Lordship's hands, I will deliver you the full and perfect relation."

Relation of the Voyage and Discovery of Hernando de Alarcón, made by order of Don Antonio de Mendoza, Viceroy of New Spain, to the very bottom of the Gulf of California, and 85 leagues up the River of Buena Guía, begun the 9 of May, 1540

CALIFORNIA

dream
mirage

night
mare?

SILENCE

I smell
silence
everywhere

clean
nice homes
smells

banks
smell
so do malls

no deodorant
odorizer
or perfume

can put way
this stink
of silence

GRANDSON'S RAGE

my grandmother
died homeless

her son's creditors
took away

her father's home
where she was born

and had lived
all of her life

they say
she lost her mind

her sight
her will

I didn't even know
for weeks

she had died alone
in Mexico

I was
18 years old

grinding
small stones

with my shoes
in L.A.

THE X IN MY NAME

the poor
signature
of my illiterate
and peasant
self
giving away
all rights
in a deceiving
contract for life

CALLEJEROS

sólo	only
estos perros	these dogs
comprenden	understand
el dolor	the pain
de las calles	of dark
oscuras	streets
mientras	while
en las casas	in homes
crujen camas	beds creak
ellos afuera	they outside
rastrean	trace what's
el olvido	forgotten
los rebeldes	forever
de siempre	rebellious
los desolados	desperados
no ladran	they don't bark
ni gruñen	or growl
a los ladrones	at thieves
lo contrario:	on the contrary
chisguetean	they spray
los muros	the walls
de los bancos	of banks
las iglesias	churches
los hoteles	hotels

MISSIONS

I visit
old missions
on the Day
of the Dead

San Diego
San Gabriel
San Juan Bautista
San Rafael

Santa Barbara
Santa Clara
Santa Inés
Santa Cruz

it usually
rains tears
white walls
start sweating

I keep on
lighting candles
hoping for a big
Indian fire

L.A. PRAYER
Abril 1992

something
was wrong
when buses
didn't come

streets
were
no longer
streets

how easy
hands
became
weapons

blows
gunfire
rupturing
the night

the more
we run
the more
we burn

o god
show us
the way
lead us

spare us
from ever
turning into
walking

matches
amidst
so much
gasoline

CHANT

nothing's
left

nothing's
gone

this is it
this is home!

RAICES

mis raíces
las cargo
siempre
conmigo
enrolladas
me sirven
de almohada

ROOTS

I carry
my roots
with me
all the time
rolled up
I use them
as my pillow

BANDERAS

trapos
imbéciles
empapados
en sangre

FLAGS

stupid
rags
soaked
in blood

SEER

I sweep
and clean
my house

I burn
the trash
get rid
of obstacles

my house
now has
no walls
no anger
or sorrow

I am resting:
my *hamaca*
is a canoe
crossing
the Milky Way

WE ARE TREES

our roots
network

with the roots
of other trees

our branches
grow

with desire
of touching

other branches

. . . . .

SOOTHER

I bite tongue
your erect
dark nipples

so your heart
won't become
another fist

EROS

no hay
llave
para tu
puerta

sólo
lengua
para tu
cerradura

EROS

there is
no key
to your
door

only
a tongue
for your
keyhole

AMOR ZURDO

they can
throw me
in jail

point
laugh
at my face

run me
out
of town

stone me
to
death

write me
off
any record

but can't
keep me
from

touching
rubbing
loving you

LOS ADOBES

son panes
de tierra
chocolate
piloncillo
hechos al sol

los muros
de adobe
acaban
en muslos
redondos

son anchos
tibios
oscuros
como
mi abuela

el viento
la lluvia
el olvido
los acaricia
los deslava

en un
descuido
se vuelven
otra vez
tierra

montoncitos
de suspiros
por
caminos
y vergeles

LOUD MAGIC

to Jorge Argueta

we are loud
way too loud

we read poems
to each other

behind closed doors
inside our room

we are now rivers
crashing

bouncing off
these walls

as indifferent
as a funeral home

we make
too much noise

we should know
better

—this time
and space—

like
rain snakes

we keep on
hissing away

the night!

*Dominican College
San Rafael, California*

"MEXICAN" IS NOT A NOUN

*to 46 UC Santa Cruz students and 7 faculty
arrested in Watsonville for showing solidarity
with 2,000 striking cannery workers who were
mostly Mexican women, October 27, 1985*

"Mexican"
is not
a noun
nor an
adjective

"Mexican"
is a life
long
low-paying
job

a check
mark on
a welfare
police
form

more than
a word
a nail in
the soul
but

it hurts
it points
it dreams
it offends
it cries

it moves
it strikes
it burns
just like
a verb

CONTINENTAL
San Francisco, Califas

las esquinas	the streets
de mi barrio	of my *barrio*
La Misión	*La Misión*
dan a	lead to
Tegucigalpa	Tegucigalpa
Guatemala	Guatemala
Managua	Managua
San Salvador	San Salvador
el mismo	the same
olor a pobre	air of poverty
el mismo pan	the same daily
de cada día	bread
la misma	the same
música	music
cosquilleando	tickling
las entrañas	inside
la vida	life
colgada	hanging
como piñata	like a *piñata*
de un hilo	by a thread

~

y palos	and blows
muchos palos	many blows
dondequiera	everywhere
muchos muertos	lots of dead
por eso aquí	that's why
el café deja	coffee leaves
anillos de luto	mourning rings
en la tazas	in cups
por eso mismo	and flags
las banderas	are used
aquí se usan	up here
de mantel	as tableclothes
por las calles	through the streets
de mi barrio	of my *barrio*
anda suelto todo	roams a whole
un continente	continent

NO GOLDEN GATE FOR US

the humid air
Tejanos
take with them
wherever they go
all of the sudden
turned into
a big tornado
ripping off
Juan Pablo's
kitchen like
Dorothy's house
flying up
the San Francisco Sky

"nobody gives
a damn
about *jotos*
dying of AIDS"
mouthed Marcos
his letter of
resignation
from the first
Latino AIDS project
inside a pocket
weighing down
his jacket:
"nobody!"

we were only
five of us
after dinner
around
a blasted kitchen

~

like old times
we formed
a circle as
tender as
our first kiss

we felt
the power
of caring
like thunder
in the desert

we landed
at the edge
of the Bay
provided
with promises
and lies and
more lies

we were
no heroes
nor too brave
we only had
ourselves
our friends
our *familias*

since
no goddamn
Golden Gate
has been laid
for us
we had no choice
but to try
crossing
the Bay's mouth

~

crossing
the Bay's mouth
by swimming
the cold and
treacherous
waters
warming
each other
side by side

seated
on the small
kitchen table
Rodrigo scribed
in his best
handwriting
the inital
manifesto
of CURAS:
"Comunidad
Unida en
Respuesta
al AIDS/SIDA"

CASA MATERNA

toqué	I knocked
a la puerta	at the door
de mi casa	of my home
de negro	a lady
una señora	in black
salió	answered
sombra	a shadow
empuñando	fisting
una escoba	a broom
sin palabras	speechless
me quedé	I kept on
mirando	staring
donde	where
se canceló	my childhood
mi infancia	was cancelled
después	after
del portazo	the door slam
seguí	I just
parado	stood there
llorando	weeping
por dentro	inside

EXTRANJERO

hoy
lo compruebo
lo padezco:

dondequiera
extranjero
soy

FOREIGNER

today
it's real
and hurts:

I am
a foreigner
everywhere

ISLA MUJERES

¿por qué
no entrar
a cualquier
casa de
pescador
y decir:
"ya llegué"

y una vez
sentados
a nuestras
anchas
suspirar:
"es una larga
historia..."

why not
just go
into any
fisherman's
house
and say:
"I'm home"

and once
seated
at our
ease
sigh:
"it's a long
story..."